10/03

John Tyler

John Tyler

Betsy Ochester

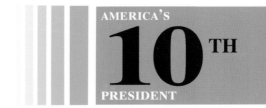

AMERICA'S

10TH

PRESIDENT

Children's Press®
A Division of Scholastic Inc.
New York / Toronto / London / Auckland / Sydney
Mexico City / New Delhi / Hong Kong
Danbury, Connecticut

Library of Congress Cataloging-in-Publication Data

Ochester, Betsy.
    John Tyler / by Betsy Ochester.
        p. cm. – (Encyclopedia of Presidents)
Includes bibliographical references and index.
  ISBN 0-516-22850-1
    1.Tyler, John, 1790–1862—Juvenile literature. 2. Presidents—United
States—Biography—Juvenile literature. I. Title. II. Series.
E397 .O28 2003
973.5'8'092—dc21
[B]   2002008799

CHILDREN'S PRESS and associated logos are trademarks and or registered
trademarks of Scholastic Library Publishing. SCHOLASTIC and associated
logos are trademarks and or registered trademarks of Scholastic Inc.
1 2 3 4 5 6 7 8 9 10 R 12 11 10 09 08 07 06 05 04 03

Contents

Chapter 1

Early Morning Surprise ———————

As dawn's soft light spread across the Virginia sky, erasing the stars for another day, a sharp rap-rap-rap broke the silence of Vice President John Tyler's house in Williamsburg, Virginia. Tyler sat up in bed, awakened by the knocking. It was only 5 A.M. Who could be calling at this hour? Tyler hurried to the door dressed in his nightshirt and cap. The vice president couldn't have been more surprised by what he learned there.

Two weary-looking men stood in the doorway. They had been traveling nearly 24 hours to bring Tyler an important message. One of the young men, Fletcher Webster, was the chief clerk of the State Department. He handed Tyler an official letter from the cabinet of President William Henry Harrison. The president was dead, after only one month in office! Without any warning, John Tyler was now the tenth president of the United States.

On April 5, 1841, Vice President John Tyler received the news that President Harrison had died. He rushed to Washington, where he was sworn in as president the next day.

Tyler awoke his family, and they discussed the situation over breakfast. He decided to leave immediately for Washington, D.C., with the messengers. Traveling by boat and horseback, they covered the 230 miles (370 kilometers) from Williamsburg in 21 hours—a near-record time.

Tyler arrived in Washington on April 6, 1841, to take on his new and unexpected responsibilities. Yet the situation was not clear. Was he really the president or merely an acting president who would hold the title until the next election? This was the first time a U.S. president had died in office, and John Tyler was the first vice president to gain the presidency under these circumstances. The Constitution was clear that the vice president would take the title, but was not so clear on what his responsibilities should be.

Well-educated and strong-willed, Tyler was an experienced politician, and he believed he was ready to assume the highest office in the land. Others, including many in his own Whig party, were not so sure. Only six months earlier, the new Whig party had gained the election of Harrison as the first Whig president. They had nominated Tyler for vice president because he was well known in Virginia, an important state to carry in the election. Now he presented a problem for the Whigs. Would he follow the party platform and work with the powerful Whig leaders in Congress?

Virginia Plantation ————————————————

That early morning visit occurred only a few days after John Tyler celebrated his 51st birthday. He was born on March 29, 1790, at his family's 1,200-acre (480-hectare) plantation, Greenway, on the tranquil banks of the James River in Charles City County, Virginia. When Tyler was born, the United States was in its infancy, too. The nation declared its independence from Great Britain only 14 years earlier, and George Washington had served as first president for less than a year.

Tyler was the sixth of eight children born to Judge John Tyler and Mary Armistead Tyler. A respected politician, Judge Tyler would serve as governor of Virginia for three terms, as speaker of the Virginia House of Delegates, and as a state and federal judge. While a student at the College of William and Mary, Judge Tyler had been a good friend and roommate of Thomas Jefferson.

Historians don't know very much about young John's childhood. We do know that when he was only seven, his mother Mary died suddenly. Judge Tyler never remarried, but seems to have raised his three sons and five daughters with love and guidance. One story reports that Judge Tyler sometimes gathered his children and children of his slaves in the shade of a large willow tree. There he entertained them by playing the violin and telling stories of his adventures during the Revolutionary War. Over the years, Judge Tyler was appointed guardian of 21 other children, many of whom may have lived at Greenway. Young John grew up surrounded by family—and many playmates.

Greenway had many things to interest curious children. In addition to the main house, the plantation had many outbuildings, including a dairy, an icehouse, a smokehouse (where meat was smoked to preserve it), two granaries, and a laundry. There were 20 horse stalls and an eight-sided pigeon house. Greenway was also home to more than forty slaves, who lived in cabins on the estate. A road lined with cedar trees led up to the gate in front of the main house. Many flowers graced the front yard, and gardens of shrubs and flowers

Tyler's father, also named John, was a Virginia plantation owner and a judge. He was a friend of Thomas Jefferson, who served as president from 1801 to 1809.

were planted behind the house. In the rich, fertile soil of the estate grew acres of wheat, corn, and tobacco.

In later years, friends of the Tyler family reported that John was much like his mother in character: polite, gentle, and well mannered. He enjoyed playing the violin and writing poetry, and he was raised to be a "southern gentleman."

On the other hand, young John also had a headstrong, stubborn streak. Another story reports that when Tyler was eleven, he led his classmates in a revolt against their schoolteacher, William McMurdo. McMurdo was an able teacher, but like many other teachers in those days, he disciplined students by striking them with a birch switch. One day McMurdo whipped many students, including Tyler's older brother Wat. At the end of the school day, Tyler led a group of boys who tied up Mr. McMurdo and locked him in the schoolhouse. Later, after a passerby untied him, the angry teacher stormed to Greenway and told Judge Tyler what had happened. The judge, knowing about McMurdo's cruel methods of discipline, was not sympathetic. He replied with a familiar Latin phrase, "*sic semper tyrannis*," which means "that's what happens to tyrants." (The phrase was also the state motto of Virginia.)

Years of Learning

A dedicated and intelligent student, Tyler entered the secondary school of the College of William and Mary in Williamsburg at age twelve, and a few years later progressed to college courses. During these years, Tyler lived with his sister Anne and her husband, James Semple, at their Williamsburg home, traveling back to Greenway on school vacations. At college he studied the classics and English literature, as well as history and economics.

Tyler and his father had more in common than just their college. John shared Judge Tyler's strong commitment to Jefferson's Democratic-Republican party, which believed in a limited federal government. This "strict constructionist" approach granted the federal government only the powers that are specifically mentioned in the Constitution. Jeffersonians believed that states should govern themselves with only limited interference by the central government. Tyler would stick to these beliefs for the rest of his life, often to the disadvantage of his political career.

John Tyler graduated from college at 17. He returned to Charles City County and began studying law. At that time, aspiring lawyers did not attend law school. Instead, they studied with a practicing lawyer, learning the profession much as an apprentice would learn a trade. John first studied law under his father's direction with additional guidance from his cousin, Chancellor Samuel Tyler. In 1809, Judge Tyler was elected governor of Virginia. Young John moved with him to Richmond, the state capital. There he continued his law studies under Edmund Randolph, who had been the *attorney general* (the nation's highest legal official) during George Washington's presidency.

Tyler received his license to practice law when he was 19. He proved to be a natural courtroom lawyer and especially enjoyed the challenge of defending criminal cases that seemed hopeless. In the courtroom he was able to polish his

The College of William and Mary, where Tyler attended secondary school and college. The Wren Building at the center was the main college building.

considerable speaking talents. He discovered that his most persuasive speeches appealed to the emotions of a jury as well as its reason. He later put this lesson to work in impassioned and influential political speeches.

Tall at just over six feet and quite thin, with blue eyes and wavy brown hair, Tyler cut an impressive figure as a public speaker. His dominant physical

Presidents Born in Virginia

The state of Virginia has been the birthplace of eight United States presidents—more than any other state. Like the first four Virginia presidents, Tyler lived and worked in Virginia throughout his life. The other three—Harrison, Taylor, and Wilson—moved to other states and pursued their careers there.

Name	Dates in Office	Virginia Birthplace	Date of Birth
George Washington	1789–97	Westmoreland County	Feb. 22, 1732
Thomas Jefferson	1801–09	Albemarle County	Apr. 13, 1743
James Madison	1809–17	Port Conway	Mar. 16, 1751
James Monroe	1817–25	Westmoreland County	Apr. 28, 1758
William Henry Harrison	1841	Charles City County	Feb. 9, 1773
John Tyler	1841–45	Charles City County	Mar. 29, 1790
Zachary Taylor	1849–50	Montebello	Nov. 24, 1784
Woodrow Wilson	1913–21	Staunton	Dec. 28, 1856

☆ ★ ☆

feature, as he was the first to admit, was his large Roman nose, with its sharp, distinguishing bump. Tyler's second wife, Julia, teasingly called it the "Tyler nose." Others were not so kind. John Quincy Adams, a political enemy of Tyler's, remarked in his diary that the shadow of Tyler's nose outstretched the shadow of the Bunker Hill Monument in Boston.

Politics and Family

Politics was in Tyler's blood. Soon he was chosen to be the representative of Charles City County in the Virginia House of Delegates, the lower house of the state legislature. Well-liked by his constituents, Tyler was elected for five consecutive terms. In one of those elections Tyler had seven opponents but still received all but five votes cast in the county.

Shortly after he graduated from college, Tyler met the lovely Letitia Christian at a party. Letitia came from another prominent Virginia family. Tyler courted her for five years, wooing the quiet, dark-haired Letitia with letters and visits to her family's plantation, Cedar Grove. John, true to the code of a Virginia gentleman, did not kiss Letitia until three weeks before their wedding—and even then it was on her hand.

The two married at Cedar Grove on March 29, 1813, John's twenty-third birthday. In the only surviving love letter written by John to Letitia during their

Letitia Christian and John Tyler were married in 1813. They had eight children. Letitia died when Tyler was serving as president.

courtship, he promised his devotion. "To ensure to you happiness is now my only object, and whether I float or sink in the stream of fortune, you may be assured of this, that I shall never cease to love you." Theirs was a loving marriage, and together they would be the parents of eight children.

After the wedding, the couple moved to Mons Sacer, a plantation next to Greenway. Two years later, they moved to a neighboring piece of land and built a new plantation home, which they called Woodburne. When John was away at Richmond or Washington on political business, Letitia usually stayed at home to raise the children and oversee the affairs of the plantation.

Tyler enjoyed telling funny stories, and the object of his humor was often himself. As a young man during the War of 1812, he became a captain of the local militia, the Charles City Rifles. The company was ordered to Williamsburg to await the approach of the British, and was housed on an upper floor in a building owned by the College of William and Mary. One night after they were in bed, they received a false report that British troops had just entered Williamsburg. Tyler and his men scrambled from their beds to meet the challenge, but in their hurry, they all fell head over heels down the dark stairway. Tyler said that injuries received in his fall were a result of his "distinguished military service."

Tyler's political career was moving ahead with distinction. In 1816, he was elected to represent a Virginia district in the U.S. House of Representatives. At 26, he was one of the youngest members of Congress.

The Growth of a Nation

Tyler's lifetime was a period of terrific growth and change in the United States. In 1803, when he was 13, the huge Louisiana Purchase nearly doubled the country's land area. The next year, the Lewis and Clark expedition explored the Rocky Mountains and the Northwest, bringing home stories and artifacts that fired the imagination of many.

A few years later, the first practical steamboats began service. Canals were being built to connect rivers and lakes so that goods could be shipped easily from one region to another. The National Road from Maryland to the west allowed settlers to cross the Appalachian Mountains on their way to the western frontier. By 1840, there were nearly 3,000 miles (4,800 km) of railroads.

The population grew by leaps and bounds, too. In 1790, the year Tyler was born, the first national census counted fewer than 4 million people. By 1840, the year Tyler was elected vice president, the fifth census reported more than 17 million.

☆ ☆ ☆

Chapter 2

Representative Tyler

John Tyler served in the U.S. House of Representatives from December 1816 to March 1821. Like most congressmen, Tyler rented a room in a modest boardinghouse when Congress was in session, usually November through March. Since a trip home took at least two days in each direction, he rarely traveled home during these months.

Because he came from a prominent Virginia family, Tyler was quickly swept into the social life of Washington. When he arrived in Washington, President James Madison, a Virginian, was serving his last months in the presidency. Tyler became a regular guest at parties hosted by the president and his wife Dolley. Tyler wrote to Letitia that he enjoyed the superb hospitality there and the champagne that was served, of which, he wrote, "you know I am very fond." But the rich

The Capitol Building as it looked around 1820. It had been rebuilt after the British set fire to it during the War of 1812.

French meals were a different story. Of the food, Tyler wrote, "I had much rather dine at home in our plain way. . . . What with their sauces and flum-flummeries, the victuals are intolerable."

D . C . = D i r t y C a p i t a l ?

When John Tyler arrived in Washington, D.C., as a young representative, the capital was not a particularly pleasant place to live. The city had been planned as the new capital of the United States in the 1790s, and the government had arrived only in 1800. Then the city was overrun by British troops during the War of 1812, and they had burned many of the public buildings, including the Capitol and the Executive Mansion.

Built on the banks of the slow-moving Potomac River, Washington was still surrounded by swamps. Malaria and other fevers were common. Cows and pigs wandered the unpaved streets. When it rained, carriage wheels sank in mud up to their hubs on the unpaved roads. In 1818, the city could not afford to buy oil to light the street lamps on Pennsylvania Avenue, and the city's main street was dark. Washington showed little sign of the beautiful city it would one day become.

In 1816, when Tyler took his seat in Congress, the Capitol and the Executive Mansion were still being rebuilt. Until December 1819, Congress met in a privately owned two-story building nearby, which was called the "Brick Capitol." The Executive Mansion received a new coat of paint to protect its soft sandstone facing and to cover places blackened by the fire. People began calling it the White House, a name that became official in 1901.

☆ ★ ☆

Henry Clay and Andrew Jackson

One of Tyler's first decisions as a representative was whether or not to vote for a large pay increase for congressmen. Salaries for congressmen were not high, and many believed that they deserved better pay. Yet it was difficult for the representatives to vote for their own pay raise. With a growing family, Tyler could use the extra money but he knew that his *constituents*, the people in his congressional district, were against the measure. In his first speech to Congress, he spoke out strongly against the bill raising salaries, and he voted against it.

Tyler always put his principles first, earning him the nickname of "Honest John." It was a name—and a trait—he prized. Another related characteristic, stubbornness, would play a large role in his political life. A friend once said of Tyler, "When he thinks he is right he is obstinate as a bull; no power on earth can move him."

In his first congressional term, Tyler met Henry Clay, a man who would be his political rival over many decades. Clay, a congressman from Kentucky, was Speaker of the House. Like Tyler, he was a Democratic-Republican, but he was the leader of a group known as the Nationalists. He favored a stronger federal government and was urging Congress to approve federal funds to build roads and other improvements to encourage trade and new settlements on the western

Henry Clay, Speaker of the House of Representatives, and Congressman Tyler disagreed on most political issues. They would clash many times during their long careers.

frontier—all policies that went against Tyler's political convictions. Tyler was civil to Clay but spoke against many of his proposals. The two men were also very different in personality. While Tyler was a quiet family man, Clay was loud and outgoing, and he had a reputation for enjoying gambling, heavy drinking, and pursuing women.

One of the biggest disagreements between Clay and Tyler was about the national bank. The first Bank of the United States was organized in 1791 by Alexander Hamilton, the secretary of the treasury under George Washington. Hamilton believed the bank would help regulate the young country's money supply and make trade and investment easier. Thomas Jefferson and his followers opposed the bank. They argued that a privately owned national bank was unconstitutional. When the first bank's charter expired in 1811, Congress refused to renew it. In 1816, though, Congress agreed to create a second Bank of the United States for another 20-year period.

By 1819, the bank was in financial trouble. Tyler was appointed to a five-person congressional committee to study the bank's problems. As he investigated the bank's records, he found that it was being mismanaged and that there was corruption among its directors. Tyler presented the findings to Congress and argued that the bank should be dissolved. Later, the Supreme Court ruled that the bank could continue, and Tyler was bitterly disappointed. The bank continued to be an emotional issue for many years, and later it would come back to haunt Tyler in the White House.

Another issue during Tyler's days as a representative involved General Andrew Jackson. In 1818, Jackson had been ordered to squelch a Seminole Indian uprising in southern Georgia. His orders allowed him to pursue the Seminole into Florida (then a possession of Spain) if necessary. Jackson not only followed his orders, he went well beyond them. Once in Florida, he captured two Spanish forts. He seized two British citizens he believed had been helping the Seminole, and he executed them. He also seized and deported Spanish officials from Florida. The United States was at peace with Britain and Spain, so Jackson's bold attacks caused deep embarrassment and even the threat of war.

Tyler wanted Congress to censure, or formally condemn, the general for his actions. However, Jackson's Florida adventure was widely popular, especially in the South and the Northwest. Secretary of State John Quincy Adams also defended Jackson, seeing that the raids might persuade Spain to sell Florida to the United States. The move to censure Jackson did not succeed. Tyler would encounter the popular general again later in his career.

General Andrew Jackson, a popular military hero, was condemned by Tyler for his invasion of Spanish Florida. Jackson was elected president in 1828 and again in 1832.

The Missouri Compromise ———————————

The most important issue during Tyler's time in the House was the Missouri question. In 1819, Missouri applied to Congress for permission to organize for statehood. It would be the first state in the new territories west of the Mississippi River, and the question was whether it should continue to permit slavery. The House passed a bill for Missouri's organization that provided for the gradual end of slavery there. The bill was voted down in the Senate, where Southern senators insisted that the federal government had no power to determine the question of slavery. They said that Missouri should decide for itself whether to be slave or free.

Soon afterward, Maine (then a part of Massachusetts) applied to become a new state, one that would prohibit slavery. Admitting one slave state and one free state at about the same time would keep the balance in the Senate between Southern and Northern senators. Still, Northerners in the House of Representatives refused to agree to admit the new state unless slavery was restricted in the other parts of the Louisiana Purchase.

The debate in Congress over the issue lasted a year, and tempers flared. Insults flew from both sides, and some congressmen even brought loaded pistols onto the House floor. Tyler wrote to his brother-in-law Henry Curtis about the debate: "Missouri is the only word ever repeated here by the politicians. You have no possible idea of the excitement that prevails here."

Finally, Speaker Henry Clay offered a compromise. Admit Missouri as a slave state and Maine as a free state, he said. Add a provision that prohibits slavery in other western territories north of a line at 36 degrees, 30 minutes latitude. (This would forbid slavery in the future states of Kansas, Nebraska, North and South Dakota, and Montana, and in parts of other states.)

Neither side liked the compromise. Congressmen from the northern states objected to any new slave states being admitted to the Union. Tyler and others from the South argued that the Constitution gave the federal government no right to regulate slavery in the territories. With tempers running high over slavery, however, many congressmen were afraid that the issue might break the country in two. They thought the compromise would at least avoid open warfare.

In the House, Tyler was a leading voice against the Missouri Compromise. Always a man of principle, he argued that it was unconstitutional. He voted against the bill. Still, the compromise passed, and it set a precedent that Congress could regulate slavery in the territories. Clay believed this compromise might settle the slavery issue, but Tyler thought otherwise. He was certain that the dispute would continue.

As the map shows, the part of the Louisiana Purchase outside of Missouri and north of the 36-degree, 30-minute line is much larger than Missouri itself. The South had gained a new slave state, but the North had gained the likelihood of many new free states in the future. The Missouri Compromise of 1820 did not solve the emotional issues of slavery and states' rights, but it did postpone a final decision for more than thirty years.

Tyler—a slave owner all his life—regarded slavery as "a dark cloud," an evil that had been inflicted on the South by the British. Still, he never freed any of his own slaves or made any attempt as president to end slavery. He seemed to hope that slavery would eventually dissolve and disappear by itself. As his biographer Robert Seager put it, Tyler wished sincerely "that slavery would just go away somehow, quietly and without fuss."

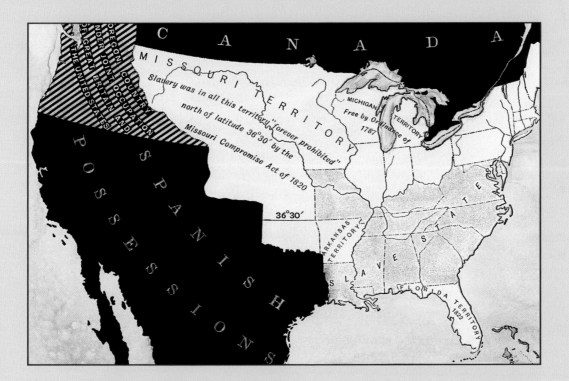

The Missouri Compromise brought Missouri into the Union as a slave state and Maine in as a free state. It also outlawed slavery in the rest of the Missouri Territory north of latitude 36° 30'.

Home to Virginia

In 1821, Tyler resigned his House seat. He was exhausted and discouraged, especially about the Missouri Compromise, which he thought damaged the authority of the Constitution. He was also ill with a digestive disorder that would trouble him for the rest of his life. He returned home to his Virginia plantation to rest and recuperate with Letitia and their growing family (three children at that time and five more to come). His health slowly improved as he enjoyed his time at home and his Charles City law practice.

Tyler couldn't stay away from politics for long, however. In 1823, he was elected to the Virginia House of Delegates. He served there for two years, resigning in 1825, when he was elected by the state's legislature to be governor.

During his term as governor Tyler proposed a number of initiatives to improve Virginia. These included a system of public schools that all classes of people could attend, and the building of roads and canals to better connect the state's regions. Many agreed that his proposals were worthwhile, but they were also expensive, and he never received the necessary funds from the state legislature.

On July 4, 1826, Thomas Jefferson died at Monticello, his estate in Virginia. Tyler's father had been a friend of Jefferson's, and Tyler had always been devoted to Jefferson's political philosophy. Appropriately, Tyler delivered a powerful public eulogy to his hero, a "brilliant and impressive oration," according to the newspaper accounts of the day.

Tyler was a popular governor. He was unanimously reelected in 1826, but a year later, his popularity propelled him beyond the governor's mansion and back to Washington. John Tyler was elected by the state legislature to the United States Senate. He resigned the governorship and returned to the national capital.

Chapter 3

Tyler and Adams

After having lived in Virginia with his family for several years, Tyler felt homesick when he arrived in Washington in December 1827 to join the Senate. As before, he moved into a room in a boardinghouse. He regularly wrote letters home, not only to Letitia, but also to his children, keeping up on their everyday life and offering fatherly advice. As he once wrote to his oldest child, Mary, "My children are my principal treasures."

Tyler sent extra money home when he could for his children to attend parties and balls. He also wrote often about their education. Unusually for that time, he was as concerned about the proper education of his daughters as he was for the education of his sons. The children studied at home with private tutors from early ages, then were

John Tyler at about the time he was serving as a senator from Virginia in 1828. He supported Andrew Jackson in the presidential election that year.

sent on to schools outside. To his young son John he wrote, "Have *hours* for reading and *minutes* for playing, and you will be a clever fellow."

Once again, Tyler also participated in the social life of Washington, almost a full-time job in itself. He attended a variety of parties, receptions, and dinners. Coming from his quiet family life on a Virginia plantation, he was sometimes shocked by the scandalous behavior of people in Washington society. That December, Tyler first saw a new dance that was sweeping American at the time—the waltz. He did not approve. He wrote to his twelve-year-old daughter Mary that the waltz was "a dance which you have never seen, and which I do not desire to see you dance. It is rather vulgar, I think."

In the presidential election of 1824, Tyler supported John Quincy Adams. Adams finished second in the voting to General Andrew Jackson, but no candidate had a majority of votes in the electoral college. Following the Constitution, the House of Representatives would make the final decision. Adams gained the support of Speaker Henry Clay, and was elected president. By the time Tyler took his seat in the Senate, Adams was nearly halfway through an unhappy term as an unpopular president.

Adams and Henry Clay were both Democratic-Republicans, but they supported a strong federal government and federal programs for roads and other improvements. Tyler, still a true believer in a limited national government, opposed the bills, repeating that such improvements were the responsibility of the states and not the federal government.

In 1828, the Adams administration passed a high *tariff* (a tax on goods imported to the United States). The tariff helped industries and merchants in the northern states because it made imported products more expensive. In the South, however, which exported cotton, tobacco, and other agricultural products, the tariff raised prices they paid for goods bought from Europe. Southerners called it the "Tariff of Abominations." Tyler voted against the tariff, but it passed.

Jackson and the Tariff

Tyler was so unhappy with the Adams administration that he decided to support Andrew Jackson for president in 1828. He said that his old adversary Jackson was the "lesser of two evils." As he wrote to a friend, "Turning to [Jackson] I may at least indulge in hope; looking on Adams I must despair."

Jackson's campaign caught the imagination of voters across the country, and he easily defeated Adams, promising to take the government out of the hands of rich merchants and bankers and give it to the common people. On his inauguration day, he invited all of his supporters to a reception at the White House. Thousands came, creating a near riot. "Old Hickory," as Jackson was known, was nearly crushed by the crowd of people hoping to get a glimpse of him. Furniture

The reception at the White House after Jackson's inauguration was open to all citizens. This artist's view is called "All Creation Going to the White House."

was broken, glasses were shattered, and fights broke out. The frightened White House servants finally moved the punch bowls out onto the lawn, and the crowd followed close behind.

While Tyler did find things to support early in the Jackson administration, he soon began to disagree with the president. When Jackson appointed friendly newspaper editors and journalists to public office, Tyler strongly disagreed with the ethics of this move. He felt that "the press, the great instrument of enlightenment of the people should not be subjected . . . to rewards and punishment."

As Jackson's first term came to an end, the Tariff of Abominations created a true national crisis—and it gave Tyler a difficult choice to make. Jackson's vice president was John C. Calhoun of South Carolina. By 1832, Calhoun had become an enemy of Jackson and resigned as vice president. Calhoun claimed that states had a right to *nullify* (refuse to enforce) a law such as the tariff that they considered unconstitutional. South Carolinians took over a federal customshouse and refused to collect the high tariff on incoming goods.

Tyler was a strong opponent of the high tariff, but he believed that a state had no right to nullify a federal law, as South Carolina was doing. He saw that if states could choose which federal laws to obey, the United States would soon no longer be united. Then President Jackson made things even more difficult.

John C. Calhoun, vice president and later senator from South Carolina, supported states' rights and opposed the hated high tariffs. When South Carolina refused to collect tariffs, President Jackson threatened to send troops to the state.

Jackson asked Congress to pass the so-called Force Bill, giving him the power to use military force against South Carolina to make them collect the tariffs. Tyler opposed the bill, and made a fiery speech against it in the Senate. Many other senators were opposed to the bill, as well. As the debate continued, Henry Clay began discussions with Calhoun, seeking a compromise on this explosive tariff issue. They finally agreed to a bill that would gradually reduce tariffs over the next ten years.

The two bills—the tariff compromise and the Force Bill—moved through Congress at about the same time. It was clear that Jackson had the votes to pass both bills. When the Force Bill came up for a vote, the senators from the southern states walked out in protest. Only Tyler, ever true to his principles, stayed. He cast the only vote against the Force Bill, which he believed gave the president dictatorial powers.

The Bank

Tyler had only begun his fight against the Jackson administration. In the election of 1832, Jackson easily defeated Henry Clay for the presidency, but Tyler was reelected to the Senate. When Congress opened in December 1833, there was a new and bitter issue to fight—the Bank of the United States.

The Second Bank of the United States was a private corporation that was partly owned by the U.S. government. It was chartered in 1816 for a period of 20 years. The federal government kept its funds in the bank, making it the largest and most important financial institution in the country—even though it was operated by private bankers who were not elected or appointed by the government.

In 1832, Henry Clay and his supporters passed a bill in Congress to renew the bank's charter when it expired in 1836. If Jackson signed the bill, he would lose many of his supporters; if he *vetoed* it (refused to sign it into law) he would be ignoring Congress and acting as a dictator. Jackson not only vetoed the bill, he sent out a powerful message defending his action. He charged that the bank was a corrupt organization that helped rich eastern merchants and bankers and damaged small farmers and tradesmen. Congress did not have the votes to *override* the veto (pass it by two-thirds majorities in both House and Senate). Jackson's stand was popular, and he was easily reelected in 1832, defeating Henry Clay himself.

In 1833, Jackson decided to take further action. Calling the bank a "monster," he said, "I will kill it!" He announced that all federal money in the bank would be withdrawn and placed in state and local banks. Tyler considered this as the act of a dictator rather than a president. Tyler also opposed the bank, but he believed that Jackson's behavior was even more dangerous than the bank. He claimed that Jackson did not have the constitutional right to destroy an institution that had been created by Congress.

Tyler became an ally of others who opposed Jackson on this issue. Henry Clay introduced a formal censure against Jackson in 1834, charging that Jackson had misused the office of president by assuming authority and power that was not given him by the Constitution. Tyler supported the censure and believed Jackson should return federal funds to the Bank of the United States. As he explained in a speech to the Senate, he wanted " the Bank to die by the law." He also warned that the president should not have ultimate power over the nation's money. "Give the president control over the purse . . . and he is every inch a king."

Disgusted by Jackson's behavior, Tyler left the Democratic party and joined the newly created Whig party. His attacks on Jackson and his support of Clay's censure resolution gained the attention of Whig leaders.

Resignation

With Tyler's support, the resolution to censure President Jackson passed in the Senate, 26 to 20, but it was never even considered by the House, where Jackson Democrats had a strong majority. Two years later, Democratic senator Thomas Hart Benton introduced a bill to expunge (erase) the censure resolution from the

The Whig Party

Formed in 1834, the Whig Party agreed on one major issue—opposition to Andrew Jackson.

The name "Whig" came from the Whig party in Great Britain, which had long worked to limit the powers of the monarchy. The American Whigs felt this was an appropriate name for their group because they aimed to stop the policies of Jackson, whom they referred to as the "United States' monarch" or "King Andrew the First."

In their hatred of Jackson, many unlikely political groups banded together. One main faction was the National Republicans, led by Henry Clay, Daniel Webster, and John Quincy Adams. They supported Clay's nationalistic "American System," which was for high tariffs, federally funded internal improvements, and a national bank. The other faction, which included John Tyler, was made up of old-fashioned Jeffersonians from the South, who believed in a limited federal government and states' rights to govern themselves with little restriction.

Thomas Ritchie, the Democratic editor of the *Richmond Enquirer*, made fun of the Whigs, saying, "They have too many persons to please. They have 'too many cooks'—and their broth may be spoiled."

In 1836, their first presidential election year as a party, the Whigs nominated several candidates, including former general William Henry Harrison from Ohio and the great Senate orator Daniel Webster from Massachusetts. John Tyler was put on some state tickets as the Whig's vice-presidential candidate. They lost the election to Jackson's vice president, Martin Van Buren, who pledged to continue Jackson's policies.

Four years later, the Whigs would have another chance at the presidency.

☆☆☆

Two powerful Massachusetts Whigs were former president John Quincy Adams (above), who was now a congressman, and Senator Daniel Webster (opposite), the most powerful speaker in Congress.

record of the Senate Journal. Tyler opposed the bill, claiming that it was impossible to erase anything from the official record of the Senate.

Tyler's stand on this issue was unpopular even in Virginia. At that time, a state legislature could instruct a senator how to vote on a particular issue. The Virginia House of Delegates instructed Tyler to vote to expunge the censure resolution. Rather than go against his principles, he resigned his seat in the Senate. He declared that "in the consciousness of my own honesty, I stand firm and erect. I worship alone at the shrine of truth and honor."

Tyler returned home to his Virginia farm, happy to again be with the most important people in his life, his wife and children. Within a few months, the family moved to Williamsburg so that Tyler could practice law in town. Once again, his private life didn't last long. In 1838 Tyler was elected to the Virginia House of Delegates, where he was chosen as speaker of the house. There he watched as the country slid into financial depression, caused in part by Jackson's banking policies. Businesses failed, farmers could not sell their crops, and many people went hungry. As president, Martin Van Buren received much of the blame for the depression.

As the 1840 election approached, the country was ready for a change. The Whigs wanted to take advantage of the nation's dissatisfaction with Van Buren—and Tyler was brought along for the ride.

Chapter 4

Tyler for Vice President

Henry Clay had long dreamed of being president. He had run and lost in 1824 and 1832. Now, in 1840, it seemed that his best chance had come. He believed that against the unpopular Martin Van Buren, almost *any* Whig could be elected. Few could deny that he and his followers were the backbone of the Whig party. That was only part of the story, however. The Whigs were still a new party and had never elected a president. Other Whigs knew that Clay had made many enemies with his support for a strong federal government and a national bank. They were worried, as one of them said, about being "stuck in the Clay." They wanted a candidate who would appeal to a wide range of voters, someone without strong views and without many enemies.

William Henry Harrison was their man. Like Andrew Jackson, Harrison was a man from the west. Like Jackson, he was recognized as a war hero, having commanded U.S. forces to victory against the Shawnee at Tippecanoe in 1811 and against the British during the War of 1812. He was tall and looked "presidential." Best of all, he had not been active in national politics, and had not stated strong views on controversial issues.

At the Whig convention, Henry Clay had the most votes on the first ballot to nominate a presidential candidate, but needed a two-thirds vote. On later ballots, his support melted away, and the convention finally chose war hero Harrison. When Clay learned of his defeat, he said angrily, "My friends are not worth the powder and shot it would take to kill them."

The Whigs knew Harrison would be popular with voters in the West, and they had strong support in the Northeast. To win the election, they needed more support in the South. To accomplish this, they looked for a southerner as their candidate for vice president. The logical choice was John Tyler. He was well known in his region, and had shown his Whig loyalty by fighting Jackson and Van Buren and by supporting Henry Clay for the presidential nomination. In the South, he was known for his support of states' rights, increasing his appeal to voters there.

The Whigs counted on Tyler to help gain southern support, but beyond that, they didn't give him much thought. Whig leaders never questioned Tyler about his views or asked him to make a pledge of loyalty to the party. In past

William Henry Harrison, a war hero like Andrew Jackson, was the Whig candidate for president in 1840. Tyler was the Whig nominee for vice president.

William Henry Harrison (1773-1841)

William Henry Harrison grew up on a family plantation in Charles City County, Virginia, not far from the Tyler plantation at Greenway. Like Tyler's father, Harrison's father Benjamin had served as governor of Virginia. Young Harrison studied to be a medical doctor, but following the sudden death of his father, he decided instead to find a career in the military.

From 1800 to 1812, he served as governor of the Indiana Territory, then the westernmost frontier. As governor, he directed dealings with Native Americans. On one hand, he tried to protect them from abuse at the hands of settlers arriving from the east. On the other hand, he negotiated treaties that paid them pennies per acre for their land and forced them to move farther west.

The Shawnee, led by their chief Tecumseh and his brother Tenskwatawa, refused to sell their land and attacked new settlements. In 1811, Harrison led a force of 1,000 men against a Shawnee village on the banks of the Tippecanoe River. After heavy fighting, Harrison and his army drove the Shawnee warriors off and burned their village. The victory was widely publicized and praised. The following year, Harrison rejoined the regular army and commanded troops in the War of 1812. He recaptured Detroit from the British and won an important victory at the Thames River in nearby Ontario, Canada.

From 1814 until his nomination, Harrison lived with his family in North Bend, Ohio, near Cincinnati. He served briefly in the U.S. House of Representatives and later in the U.S. Senate, but lost more elections than he won. To earn a living for his family, he served as clerk to a local court in Cincinnati. Beginning in 1832, he campaigned in his region for higher office, aiming particularly at the presidency. When the Whigs nominated him for president in 1840, Harrison was 67 years old.

☆☆☆

administrations, the vice president had been nearly invisible, and the Whigs expected that Tyler, too, would stand quietly in the background after the election.

"Tippecanoe and Tyler, Too!"

The campaign of 1840 was different from all previous presidential campaigns. Thanks to Whig campaign managers, it reached nearly every village and town in the United States, promising entertainment and fun. Many people had been suffering from economic hard times, and they seemed ready to enjoy a circuslike campaign that featured parades, singing, and amusing political insults.

Harrison gained a nickname, "Old Tippecanoe," reminding voters of his victory on the Tippecanoe River over the Shawnee nearly thirty years earlier. The campaign slogan included Tyler's name, and it rhymed. "Tippecanoe and Tyler, Too!" rang from one side of the country to the other.

Early in the campaign, a Democratic newspaper ridiculed Harrison, saying that if he had a keg of hard cider (an inexpensive alcoholic drink popular in the West) and a pension, he would stay in his log cabin rather than run for president. The insult gave the campaign its two great symbols—the cider keg and the humble log cabin. The symbols appeared in crudely printed campaign sheets and were worked into embroidery and quilting designs. Parades often featured a miniature log cabin pulled on a wagon. Campaign rallies offered free hard cider

A Whig rally in 1840 features a parade with a log cabin on a wagon with the slogan "Tippecanoe and Tyler Too."

to the crowds. Whig campaigners compared Harrison to President Martin Van Buren, who was portrayed as a richly dressed champagne-drinker who lounged late in bed on silk pillows in the White House.

For the first time, many women got involved in a presidential campaign. They were known as Harrison Ladies or Log Cabin Belles. They cooked for rallies, made handicrafts with the log cabin theme, and marched in parades. Even though they couldn't vote, they chanted along with the crowds, "Tippecanoe and Tyler, Too!"

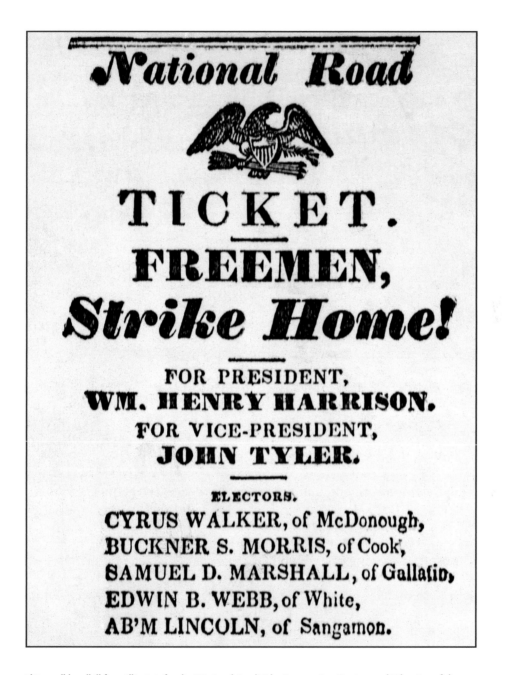

This small handbill from Illinois is for the "National Road Ticket" supporting Harrison and Tyler. One of the electors is a young Illinois lawyer named Abraham Lincoln.

Early in the campaign, a few Whig supporters fashioned a huge ball ten feet (three meters) high, which they rolled down the street in a parade with the slogan "Keep the Ball Rolling for Harrison." Rolling a big ball for Harrison became a fad, and many were made in different parts of the country. One group claimed to have rolled their ball more than 400 miles (640 km)!

Newspapers reported that many people named their babies or pets after the Whig candidates. In the West, it was even reported that when hens laid eggs they cackled, "Tip-tip! Tip-tip! Tyler."

Tyler, ever the Virginia gentleman, was uncomfortable with the "folksy" nature of the campaign. He was a talented speaker in front of Congress, but he never felt comfortable speaking to masses of "ordinary people." He spent as little time as possible campaigning. As election day neared he did travel a little, giving purposely vague speeches in Ohio, Virginia, and Pennsylvania.

The campaign generated great enthusiasm for the Whigs through its images and cheerfulness, yet it didn't say much about the candidates themselves. No one observed that both Harrison and Tyler had grown up on prosperous plantations in Virginia, the sons of influential landowners. By contrast, Van Buren was a self-made man from a middle-class background. Campaigners also didn't mention that Harrison and Tyler were an odd political pair to share a ticket. Harrison and many Whigs were eager to put through a nationalist program, reestablishing a national bank and creating a more powerful federal government. Tyler was a strict constructionist who didn't favor the nationalist program and had often spoken against it.

Looking back at the campaign later, many observers saw its flaws. Philip Hone, once mayor of New York City, wrote in his diary of the "Tippecanoe and Tyler, Too!" slogan, "There was rhyme, but no reason in it." Carl Schurz, a biographer of Henry Clay, wrote nearly fifty years later, "There has probably never been a presidential campaign of more enthusiasm and less thought."

Still, the campaign succeeded in attracting voters. More than 80 percent of the nation's eligible voters turned out—in 1836, only 58 percent had voted. Harrison and Tyler gained about 1.2 million votes to 1.1 million for Van Buren. In the electoral college, they won by a wide margin, carrying 19 states with 234 votes to Van Buren's 7 states with only 60 votes. The Whigs also gained control of the House of Representatives and won a majority of seats in the Senate. As Philip Hone later observed, "General Harrison was *sung* into the presidency."

Ironically, one of the seven states won by Van Buren was Virginia. Tyler, who had been nominated to help carry the southern states, did not carry his home state.

Sung into Office

Rhymes and songs became great new tools in the campaign of 1840. Men, women, and children across the country might have little understanding of the politics, but they could all remember "Tippecanoe and Tyler, Too!"

Whig enthusiasts across the country sang:

> And we'll vote for Tyler, therefore,
>
> Without a why or wherefore.

Paraders belted out their loyalty across the nation with lyrics such as:

> What has caused this great commotion, motion,
>
> Our country through?
>
> It is the ball a-rolling on,
>
> For Tippecanoe and Tyler too,
>
> Tippecanoe and Tyler too.

Other songs concentrated on the opponent, President Martin Van Buren:

> Van, Van
>
> Is a used-up man

and:

> Let Van from his coolers of silver drink wine,
>
> And lounge on his cushioned settee,
>
> Our man on a buckeye bench can recline,
>
> Content with hard cider is he.

Of all this musical commotion, the *New York Evening Post*, a pro-Van Buren newspaper, said: "We could meet the Whigs on the field of argument and beat them without effort. But when they lay down the weapons of argument and attack us with musical notes, what can we do?"

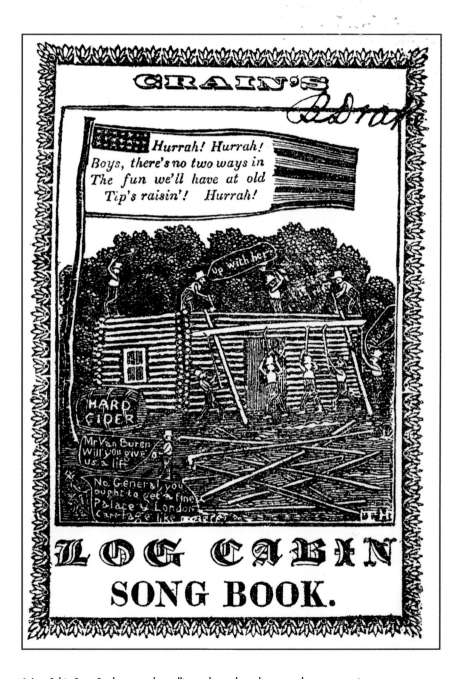

A *Log Cabin Song Book* was used at rallies and parades, where crowds sang campaign songs set to familiar tunes.

A New Administration

After the election, Harrison was pestered day and night by Whigs seeking appointment to his cabinet and other government positions. Tyler played no part in selecting Harrison's cabinet—no one asked him to. Henry Clay chose to remain in the Senate, hoping to use his power there to gain the presidency in four years' time. Daniel Webster of Massachusetts became secretary of state.

Inauguration day, March 4, 1841, was cold and raw. Huge crowds—some 50,000 people—turned out to cheer on Harrison and Tyler. The new president

The inauguration of Harrison and Tyler in Washington on March 4, 1841.

delivered the longest inauguration address in history, lasting an hour and forty minutes, wearing neither hat nor overcoat. One historian called it the "worst in American history."

Left weakened by the campaign and meetings with office seekers, the 68-year-old Harrison seemed to have little energy for his new job. Late in March, he caught pneumonia, and on April 4, one month after his inauguration, he died. He was the first president to die in office.

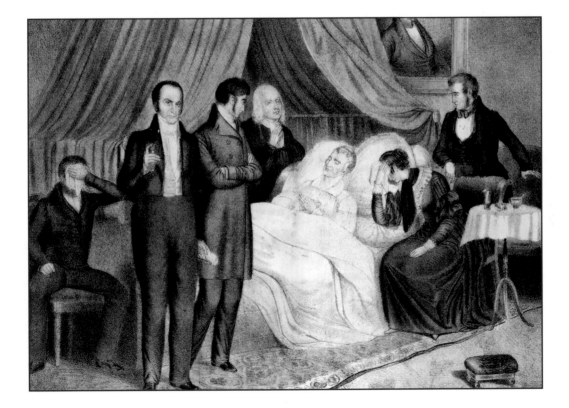

President Harrison died of pneumonia in the White House less than a month after he took office.

Tyler was at home in Williamsburg. As vice president, his only official duties were to preside over the Senate, and the Senate would not begin its business until late in the year. Then he received the shocking news of Harrison's death. He returned immediately to Washington. Letitia and the children would follow.

To Be or Not to Be President?

The Constitution says, "In case of the removal of the President from office, or of his death, resignation, or inability to discharge the powers and duties of the said office, the same shall devolve on the Vice-President."

Is the vice president to take on the office of president or only the duties of the office? Some political leaders argued that he should serve as "acting president," holding the place of the departed president until the end of the term, when a new elected president could take office.

From the beginning, Tyler believed he was to take over the office of president with all its powers and duties. He insisted on taking on the full responsibilities of the office. His actions as president set an important precedent, which has been followed by later vice presidents who were elevated to the presidency when a president died or resigned.

☆ ★ ☆

President Tyler ───────

Tyler arrived in Washington, D.C., in the early morning of April 6, 1841. After checking into Brown's Indian Queen Hotel, Tyler called a meeting of the cabinet at his hotel. He asked each cabinet member one by one if he would continue to serve. Each said yes. Then he arranged for William Cranch, chief justice of the U.S. Circuit Court of the District of Columbia, to administer the oath of office. It was now official: John Tyler was the tenth president of the United States.

John Tyler served as president for all but one month of Harrison's term.

The Whigs were encouraged that Tyler kept the members of Harrison's cabinet. They assumed he would cooperate with Clay and the other Whig leaders, and would push through their agenda. At age 51—the youngest man to become president up to then—Tyler was a bright and experienced politician. He was also charming, courteous, and warm. Even his enemies were charmed by him.

Tyler walked with the cabinet members in Harrison's funeral procession on April 7. Then on April 14, he and his family moved into the White House. Two of Tyler's sons, Robert and John Jr., both lawyers, worked in the Tyler administration—Robert in the U.S. Land Office and John as his father's private secretary. A paralyzing stroke two years earlier had left Letitia an invalid. In the White House she stayed upstairs, out of the public rooms. She made an appearance in the downstairs of the mansion only once, on the occasion of her daughter Elizabeth's wedding.

Since Letitia was unable serve as hostess at White House events, Robert's wife, Priscilla Cooper Tyler, took over the job. An accomplished stage actress, she was extremely successful at coordinating, planning, and hosting the many dinners, balls, and parties. The social graces of Priscilla and President Tyler were noted in the press. In the *New York Herald* on December 18, 1841, the president was described as being able to "put his guests at ease, and throw a charm over the hospitalities of the White House."

During the first regular meeting of the cabinet, Secretary of State Daniel Webster explained how Harrison had organized his work. Harrison planned to ask the cabinet its opinion on every important question and to go along with the view of the majority. Tyler politely replied that he would not work this way. While he valued their opinions, the final decision would be his own. "I am the president and I shall be held responsible for my administration," Tyler said. "I shall be

Dolley Madison, widow of former president James Madison, advised Tyler on planning formal receptions at the White House. Then in her 70s, she was still widely admired as a gracious hostess.

pleased to avail myself of your counsel and advice. But I can never consent to being dictated to as to what I shall or shall not do."

The Whig leaders began to worry.

Tyler vs. Clay

Clay was already at work planning the Whigs' agenda in Congress, and he expected the president's support. With his so-called American System, Clay wanted to create a "nation" out of the confederation of individual states, and he wanted Congress to have control over it. Tyler and most of his fellow Southern Whigs disagreed with Clay's agenda. They thought that the United States should remain a confederation of states with a limited central government. Tyler believed that is what the Constitution mandated.

His disagreements with Clay made Tyler's first year a stormy one. When the Whigs realized that Tyler would not be their puppet, tempers flared. Whigs in Congress called Tyler "His Accidency," for the way he assumed office. Soon he acquired another nickname—the "Veto President."

At first, Tyler tried to find a compromise with Clay. Realizing the need to revive the nation's sagging economy, he agreed to discuss the issue of a national bank. He supported a Whig plan for a district bank, a bank in Washington incorporated by Congress, with branches in those states whose legislatures allowed it. Webster also supported this compromise, saying that it was better to agree on some bank than on no bank at all. But Clay wanted no compromise at all. He wanted a new Bank of the United States.

During a conversation in the president's office, Clay told Tyler that the Whigs would not accept the District Bank plan. Tyler lost his normal tact and raised his voice. "Then go to your end of the capital and perform your duty as you think proper. So help me God, I shall do mine at this end—as I shall think proper."

Clay and the Whigs proceeded with their plan for a new national bank, gaining a majority in both the House and the Senate. On August 7, 1841, the bank bill was presented to Tyler for his signature. A Whig representative, John Botts, wrote to Tyler on August 10, "If you can reconcile this bill to yourself, all is sunshine and calm: your administration will be met with the warm, hearty, zealous support of the whole Whig party." But Tyler could not agree to something that he felt went against the Constitution. On August 16, he returned the bill with his veto.

Late that night about thirty people gathered outside the White House. They fired shotguns, blew trumpets, and chanted such things as "Down with

Henry Clay, the most powerful Whig, hoped to "manage" Tyler's presidency. They soon became enemies when Tyler vetoed Clay's bills establishing a new national bank.

Tyler," and "A bank! A bank! Down with the veto!" They hurled stones through the first floor windows, frightening Letitia, who watched from upstairs. Tyler and his servants guarded the doors with guns.

The next day in Congress, Clay gave a mean-spirited speech in the Senate chamber about his "former friendship" with Tyler.

The Whigs decided to push ahead with their plan with or without the president. Clay made a few minor changes to the bank bill and again it passed in both houses. He was sure that Tyler would not have the courage to veto a second bank bill. He told a friend, "Tyler dares not resist. I will drive him before me!"

Tyler did resist. He vetoed the second bank bill on September 9, 1841. He said that he would rather uphold the Constitution "even though I perish . . . than to win the applause of men by a sacrifice of my duty and my conscience."

By vetoing the bank bills, Tyler ruined the Whigs' dream of a Bank of the United States—and he also ruined his own political future. The response to the second veto was more outrageous and violent than the response to the first. Whig leaders organized demonstrations and protests across the country. They burned Tyler in effigy. Hundreds of letters arrived at the White House, some threatening assassination.

The cabinet responded in their own way. On the afternoon of Saturday, September 11, a cabinet meeting was scheduled at the White House. Instead of arriving for the meeting, each secretary, except for Daniel Webster, sent in his resignation by messenger. Clay had carefully planned this mass resignation to punish Tyler for his vetoes. The Whigs thought this would be a killer blow to Tyler. Congress was to adjourn on Monday, and it was necessary for the Senate to confirm new cabinet appointments. If Tyler couldn't come up with a new cabinet, he would have to govern without cabinet advice for months and might choose to resign instead.

Tyler was not ruffled, however. He learned of the cabinet's plan ahead of time and had already identified new cabinet members. He accepted the resignations, then announced his new appointments. Unable to object to Tyler's choices, the Senate approved the new cabinet before adjourning. Tyler now had a handpicked cabinet more in line with his states' rights beliefs.

Whig extremists were determined to get the last word on the matter, however. On Monday, September 13, the last day of that session of Congress, a group of about fifty Whig Congress members met in Capitol Square. They read a manifesto denouncing Tyler's conduct. Then the group formally expelled Tyler from the Whig party. In Clay's famous words, Tyler was now "a president without a party."

Chapter 5

"At War with Everybody"

When the next session of Congress began in December 1841, Henry Clay and his supporters were still seething. Wanting to further punish Tyler for his vetoes, they attempted to block all of Tyler's legislation that session. As a result, the lawmakers stayed in session longer—269 days—than ever before, but accomplished little and became known as the "do-nothing Congress."

During this trying time, Tyler faced a potentially violent situation in Rhode Island. The state's constitution gave the right to vote only to white men who owned a large amount of property. As a result, only 40 percent of Rhode Island's white male population was eligible to vote in 1842. Thomas Dorr, a lawyer, led those without property who demanded that the legislature end voting restrictions. When the assembly refused, Dorr and his followers occupied a state armory in Providence. The uprising became known as Dorr's Rebellion.

The governor of Rhode Island, Sam King, asked President Tyler for federal troops to put down the uprising, as provided for in the U.S. Constitution. Tyler wanted the dispute resolved, but not by the use of force. As the situation grew worse, Tyler warned the rebels to disperse and threatened to send in federal troops if violence broke out. Finally, the rebels left the armory peacefully. The following year, Dorr was elected governor, and a new state constitution granted voting rights to most white men. Tyler was later praised for his skillful handling of a potentially explosive situation.

The Whig leaders had many powerful friends at prominent newspapers. After his vetoes, the press was filled with negative stories about Tyler's political views and his character. Gradually, the drumbeat of criticism turned public sentiment against him. To make things worse, the economy was still depressed, and like Van Buren before him, Tyler received the blame. When an epidemic of influenza (then called "the grippe") swept the country in 1842, it became known as the "Tyler grippe."

In 1842, Tyler invited American writer Washington Irving and British novelist Charles Dickens to a reception at the White House. Dickens wrote of Tyler:

He looked somewhat worn and anxious—as well he might: being at war with everybody—but the expression of his face was mild and pleasant, and his manner was remarkably unaffected, gentlemanly, and agreeable. I thought that, in his whole carriage and demeanor, he became his station singularly well.

Foreign affairs was one area where Tyler could work without the daily approval of Congress. One of his successes was the Webster-Ashburton Treaty of 1842. For years, the United States and Great Britain had been disputing the Maine-Canada boundary. In June 1842, negotiations between Secretary of State Daniel Webster and Lord Ashburton of Great Britain were near a breakdown. Tyler met with Ashburton and eased his concerns about U.S. intentions. Ashburton, impressed by the president's polished manners and his message, agreed to continue negotiations with Webster. The Webster-Ashburton Treaty was finally concluded and signed. It fixed the border between Maine and Canada, and set the U.S.-Canada boundary from Lake of the Woods in present-day Minnesota to the Rocky Mountains. It also committed the United States to engage in naval patrols off the western coast of Africa to help Britain stop the slave trade.

Tyler also took an interest in the Pacific region. The Treaty of Wanghai (1844) opened trading between the United States and China for the first time.

The States During the Presidency of John Tyler

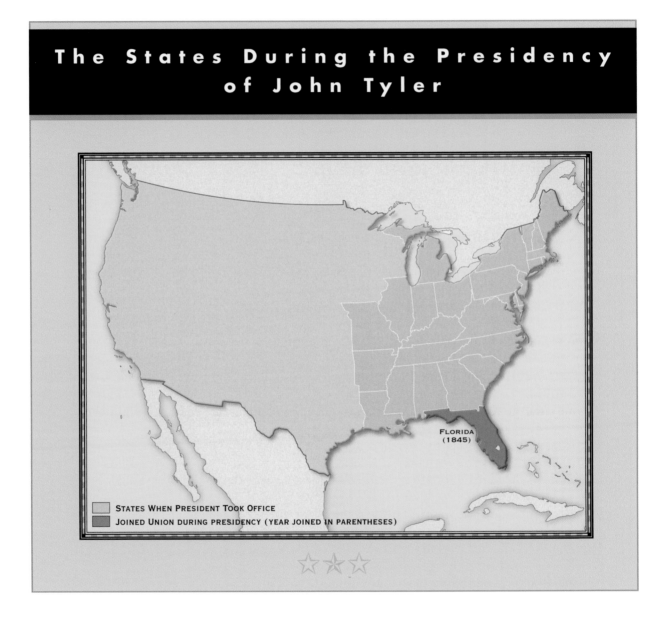

FLORIDA
(1845)

☐ STATES WHEN PRESIDENT TOOK OFFICE
■ JOINED UNION DURING PRESIDENCY (YEAR JOINED IN PARENTHESES)

When Britain and France showed interest in seizing the Sandwich Islands (present-day Hawaii), Prince Haolilio appealed to Tyler for help. Tyler invoked the Monroe Doctrine, which warned European nations against establishing colonies in the Americas. Britain and France withdrew, and the islands remained under U.S. influence, becoming a state in 1959.

In domestic affairs, Tyler continued to battle Clay and the Whig majority in Congress. Clay supported a bill that would require the federal government to share with the states money it collected from the sale of land to western settlers. The bill was popular in Congress since it brought new funds to states, but it would also reduce the federal government's income, making it difficult to balance the federal budget. Clay supported another bill calling for higher tariffs to replace the money the government would lose by sharing the land-sale money. When both bills passed, they came to Tyler's desk for his signature.

Once again, Tyler used the veto, refusing to sign either bill. The tariffs proposed were too high, he said. If the federal government kept the money from land sales, tariffs could be lower. This time he got his way. Congress was forced to pass another bill calling for a slight increase in tariffs and no sharing of land-sale money with the states. Tyler signed this bill—the Tariff Act of 1842. It brought in enough money to balance the federal budget by the end of his administration.

In March 1842, Henry Clay resigned from the Senate, so that he could prepare to run again for president in 1844. In the 1842 elections, the Whigs lost many congressional seats. They kept a small majority in the Senate, but lost their majority in the House of Representatives. Tyler saw these election results as a sign that the voting public agreed with his vetoes of Whig bills.

The Whigs were still not resigned to Tyler's presidency. In January of 1843, Representative John Botts introduced a resolution calling for the impeachment of Tyler—charging him with "high crimes and misdemeanors" in the hope of removing him from office. It was the first impeachment resolution ever offered against a president. Botts and other Whigs claimed that Tyler's use of vetoes and other actions were dictatorial and unconstitutional. The resolution received wide publicity, but because the charges were vague and unfounded, the House never acted on it.

Meanwhile, Letitia's health declined rapidly. On September 10, 1842, she died. Tyler and the children mourned her death, and even Tyler's enemies expressed their sympathy. An obituary in the Washington *Intelligencer* said Letitia was "loving and confiding to her husband, gentle and affectionate to her children, kind and charitable to the needy and afflicted."

Tyler helped deal with his grief and loneliness by buying and remodeling a plantation home on the banks of the James River. The house, called Walnut

Question of privilege.

Mr. Botts, as a privileged subject, submitted the following:

" I do impeach John Tyler, Vice President, acting as President of the United States, of the following high crimes and misdemeanors:

" 1st. I charge him with gross usurpation of power and violation of law, in attempting to exercise a controlling influence over the accounting officers of the Treasury Department, by ordering the payment of accounts of long standing that had been by them rejected for want of legal authority to pay, and threatening them with expulsion from office unless his orders were obeyed; by virtue of which threat, thousands were drawn from the public Treasury without the authority of law.

" 2d. I charge him with a wicked and corrupt abuse of the power of appointment to and removal from office: first, in displacing those who were competent and faithful in the discharge of their public duties, only because they were supposed to entertain a political preference for another; and, secondly, in bestowing them on creatures of his own will, alike regardless of the public welfare and his duty to the country.

" 3d. I charge him with the high crime and misdemeanor of aiding to excite a disorganizing and revolutionary spirit in the country, by placing on the records of the State Department his objections to a law, as carrying no constitutional obligation with it; whereby the several States of this Union were invited to disregard and disobey a law of Congress which he himself had sanctioned and sworn to see faithfully executed, from which nothing but disorder, confusion, and anarchy, can follow.

" 4th. I charge him with being guilty of a high misdemeanor, in retaining men in office for months after they have been rejected by the Senate as unworthy, incompetent, and unfaithful, with an utter defiance of the public will and total indifference to the public interests.

" 5th. I charge him with the high crime and misdemeanor of withholding his assent to laws indispensable to the just operations of Government, which involved no constitutional difficulty on his part; of depriving the Government of all legal means of revenue; and of assuming to himself the whole power of taxation, and of collecting duties of the people, without the authority or sanction of law.

" 6th. I charge him with an arbitrary, despotic, and corrupt abuse of the veto power, to gratify his personal and political resentments against the Senate of the United States for a constitutional exercise of their prerogative in the rejection of his nominees to office, with such evident marks of inconsistency and duplicity as leave no room to doubt his disregard of the interests of the people and his duty to the country.

" 7th. I charge him with gross official misconduct, in having been guilty of a shameless duplicity, equivocation, and falsehood, with his late Cabinet and Congress, which led to idle legislation and useless public expense, and by which he has brought such dishonor on himself as to disqualify him from administering the Government with advantage, honor, or virtue, and for which alone he would deserve to be removed from office.

" 8th. I charge him with an illegal and unconstitutional exercise of power, in instituting a commission to investigate past transactions under a former administration of the custom-house in New York under the pretence of

From the proceedings of the House of Representatives, these are the first of nine articles of impeachment against Tyler proposed by Congressman Botts. The House never voted on the accusations.

Grove, would be Tyler's home for the rest of his life. In early 1843, he playfully renamed it "Sherwood Forest," after Robin Hood's legendary hideout. Tyler identified with Robin Hood since he himself was considered an outlaw—by the Whig party.

Texas

Tyler took up another cause during the second half of his administration—the annexation of Texas. Texas had declared its independence from Mexico on March 2, 1836, and had expressed interest in becoming a state. Tyler believed the United States should *annex* Texas (make it part of the United States). He believed it would be a great stepping-stone in the United States' westward expansion and Pacific trading. He also worried that if the United States did not annex Texas, the Lone Star Republic could ally itself with Britain so that the United States would face British power both to the south and the north.

Annexation was not popular with many Whigs, however. They believed that it was sure to lead to war with Mexico, which still claimed the territory. Northern Whigs were also against annexation because Texas would almost certainly apply for admission to the Union as a slave state, bringing on another crisis over slavery. Secretary of State Daniel Webster was strongly opposed to annexing Texas. When Webster resigned in 1843, however, Tyler chose a new secretary of state who favored annexation. His choice was Abel P. Upshur, a close friend who had been secretary of the navy.

In December 1843, Upshur took a poll of Congress. He reported to Tyler that two-thirds of the Congress favored the annexation of Texas and would vote accordingly. Tyler was pleased and began talks with the president of Texas, Sam Houston. Before negotiations were complete, however, tragedy struck.

Tragedy and a Happy Ending

On February 28, 1844, a bright and beautiful winter day, Tyler and about 350 other politicians and dignitaries boarded the USS *Princeton* for a cruise on the Potomac River. The pride of the navy, the *Princeton* was the first steam-powered warship made of iron. President Tyler, a strong supporter of the U.S. Navy, had helped get money for new ships and equipment, including the *Princeton*.

The highlight of the trip was to be the firing of the "Peacemaker," the largest naval gun in the world. The crowd stood on deck to watch the captain fire and cheered the booming result. Then they went belowdecks for a banquet. As the ship cruised past George Washington's Mount Vernon plantation, it was suggested that the Peacemaker be fired again in honor of the first president. The captain and many guests climbed back on deck. Tyler stayed below to listen to his son-in-law, who was singing for the guests.

Suddenly there was a massive explosion. The Peacemaker had blown up, killing eight and injuring many more. Among the dead were two of Tyler's cabinet—Secretary of the Navy Thomas Gilmer and Secretary of State Upshur. Also killed in the explosion was David Gardiner, a wealthy New Yorker who was on the cruise with his beautiful young daughter Julia.

John Tyler had been courting Julia since he met her at a White House party the previous winter. After the explosion, Tyler carried the terrified Julia to a rescue boat, then went back to the ship to help with the dead and injured.

From this tragic scene, some happiness bloomed. Seven weeks after the explosion on the *Princeton*, Julia agreed to marry the president. Tyler wrote a letter to Julia's mother, Juliana McLachlan Gardiner, asking formally for Julia's hand in marriage. "It will be the study of my life to advance her happiness by all and every means in my power," he wrote. Juliana agreed to the wedding, but she expressed concern that Tyler might not be able to provide for Julia in the style she was used to as part of a wealthy family.

Julia Gardiner and John Tyler were married on the morning of June 26, 1844, in a private ceremony at the Episcopal Church of the Ascension on Fifth Avenue in New York City. News of the wedding in the newspapers the next day surprised the country, and shocked many. Julia was 23 years old, and John Tyler was 54.

The explosion on the steamship *Princeton* on February 28, 1844, killed two of Tyler's cabinet members and the father of his future wife. Tyler, who was below deck, was not injured.

The Rose of Long Island

Julia Gardiner grew up amidst wealth and luxury on New York's Long Island. Restless with her small-town upbringing, young Julia once posed for an advertisement for a New York City department store. The ad showed a drawing of her strolling in front of the store, and the caption "Rose of Long Island." Her parents were humiliated—people of wealth and good family simply did not appear in advertisements.

In the winter of 1842-43, her father, who had served in the New York State Senate, took Julia and her sister Margaret to spend a few months in Washington. The lovely Julia enjoyed a constant round of social events and parties. Some of the city's most eligible bachelors paid court to her, but it was the tall, charming president who succeeded in winning her heart. After the wedding, Julia relished her job as first lady, serving as hostess at many galas and parties. At one, she introduced the waltz to the White House—the same dance that Tyler, years earlier, had been appalled by. This time Tyler didn't mind it and even waltzed himself.

Julia Gardiner and President Tyler were married in 1844. She was 30 years younger than he, but they had seven children and lived happily until Tyler's death in 1862.

John and Julia Tyler had seven children. After John Tyler died in 1862, Julia never remarried. During the Civil War, she took her young children to live in the safety of her mother's house in Staten Island, New York, but she always supported the South. After the war, she returned to Virginia, where she lived the rest of her years. She died on July 10, 1889, at the age of 69.

☆ ☆ ☆

By all accounts, the age difference was not a problem. Julia and John Tyler would remain happily devoted to one another until Tyler's death. Tyler wrote to his daughter Mary about his new bride, "Julia Gardiner, the most lovely of her race . . . is all that I could wish her to be, the most beautiful woman of the age and at the same time the most accomplished."

The Fight Continues

After Secretary of State Upshur's death on the *Princeton*, Tyler lost ground on the annexation of Texas. Unknown to Tyler, his old friend Representative Henry Wise had offered the secretary of state position to John Calhoun. Although Calhoun was a friend of Tyler's, he had strong proslavery views. Tyler knew this would make it more difficult to get approval for annexation of Texas, reminding people that Texas would likely become a slave state.

At the same time, Tyler's term of office was running out. He knew there was no chance that Whigs or Democrats would nominate him to run in 1844. Thinking of his legacy as president, Tyler decided to form a third party whose main theme was annexing Texas. Running with the slogan "Tyler and Texas," he knew he had no chance of winning, but he believed he might be able to influence the other candidates.

The Whigs had no use for Tyler in the election of 1844. In this cartoon, Whig candidate Henry Clay is auctioning off "old" politicians. Tyler is shown as an ass that bleats "Veto! Veto!" A man in the crowd says, "I don't like that ass, he kicks."

In his battle for Texas, Tyler had an unlikely ally—Andrew Jackson. As the Democrats met to choose a candidate, Jackson came to the decision that Texas should be annexed. He threw his support to James K. Polk, a fellow Tennessean who also favored annexation. When the Democrats put the annexation of Texas in their platform, President Tyler withdrew from the race. The Whigs nominated Henry Clay. Clay tried to avoid the issue of Texas and it hurt his campaign. Polk was elected by a small margin.

Tyler saw the election of Polk as proof that the nation was in favor of annexing Texas. When Congress met in December after the election, Tyler demanded swift action to annex Texas before he left office. Julia joined in the fight. She dined with and lobbied congressmen and their wives to ask them for their support on the Texas issue.

In February, the resolution to annex Texas passed. On March 1, only three days before he left office, Tyler signed the measure into law. As a token of his appreciation for her help and support, Tyler gave Julia the golden pen he used to sign the measure. Julia cherished this gift. She had the pen made into a necklace, and was buried with it around her neck.

Julia's final White House party, held on February 18, 1845, was her grandest yet. She invited 2,000 guests to mark the end of Tyler's presidency; 3,000 showed up. The red-coated Marine band played. Six hundred candles lit the four rooms of the party, shedding flickering light on the many dancers. Barrels of wine and eight dozen bottles of champagne were consumed. As the last guests were leaving, Tyler joked, "They cannot say now that I am a president without a party!"

Still hoping for fair recognition of his administration's many achievements, Tyler said in his parting speech, "In 1840 I was called from my farm to undertake the administration of public affairs, and I foresaw that I was called to a

In 1844, while the Whigs were fighting among themselves, the Democrats nominated James K. Polk for president, and he was elected, defeating Henry Clay. This is his inauguration in 1845.

bed of thorns. I now leave that bed which has afforded me little rest, and eagerly seek repose in the quiet enjoyments of rural life. I rely on future history, and on the candid and impartial judgement of my fellow citizens, to award me the meed [honor] due to honest and conscientious purposes to serve my country."

It would be many decades before Tyler got such public recognition.

Life at Sherwood Forest

The years John Tyler spent with Julia in retirement at Sherwood Forest were, no doubt, among the happiest in his life. There they raised their seven children—five boys and two girls—and Tyler supervised the plantation's production of wheat and corn. For fun, John and Julia enjoyed entertaining neighbors and guests with dinner banquets and dancing. On warm summer evenings, they would sit outside on the piazza, where Tyler would play his fiddle and Julia would strum her guitar and sing. They wrote love poems to one another throughout their marriage.

During his retirement, Tyler wrote letters to friends extolling the virtues of his family. His new children, he said, kept him feeling young. "Thus it is that my old age is enlivened by the scenes of my youth—and these precious buds and blossoms almost persuade me

Tyler bought the Sherwood Forest plantation during his presidency and lived there with his family in retirement. The home is still occupied by Tyler's descendants.

that the springtime of life is still surrounding me." John Tyler had more children than any president before or after: 15 in total, one of whom died in infancy. Many descendants of the 14 children live in the same area of tidewater Virginia where Tyler himself spent much of his life.

Sherwood Forest was home to President John Tyler until his death in 1862. The plantation, now a National Historic Landmark, is still owned and lived in by Tyler's direct family. The current house was built in 1730. After Tyler bought Sherwood Forest, he and Julia added a 68-foot-long (21 meters) ballroom to the house in order to accommodate the popular dance at the time, the Virginia reel. The ballroom expanded the length of the house to more than 300 feet (91 m), about the length of a football field. That made it the longest frame house in America, a distinction it still holds today.

Sherwood Forest was slightly damaged by Union soldiers during the Civil War, but survived. Julia repaired the damage and lived in the house until her death. The house underwent a historic restoration in the mid-1970s. Today visitors are welcome to visit the grounds, and tours of the house may be made by appointment. Visitors can stroll on acres of terraced gardens and lawns, and see six original outbuildings. The grounds contain more than eighty types of trees, including one of the oldest known ginkgo trees in the United States—a gift to Tyler from Captain Matthew Perry on his return from China in the 1850s.

A magazine illustration shows Tyler at a party he arranged for children. He enjoyed being around children and fathered 15 of his own, more than any other president.

The Search for Peace

After leaving Washington, Tyler never lost interest in politics, following the action closely from his home in Virginia. In 1844, he left the Whig party and returned to the Democratic party, where he stayed for the rest of his days.

In the 1850s, the threat of secession and war between the North and South came ever closer. As Tyler had predicted, the Missouri Compromise of 1820 postponed the conflicts between regions, but had not solved them. As he had in the nullification crisis, Tyler favored saving the Union and desperately hoped that a compromise between the North and South could be reached. In November 1860, the election of Abraham Lincoln of the antislavery Republican party brought the crisis to a head. By the end of the year, South Carolina *seceded* from the Union (left the United States). Several other states were debating whether to secede. As a last try at compromise, the Virginia legislature proposed a peace conference, and Tyler supported the idea.

The Peace Convention was held in Washington, D.C., in February 1861, less than a month before Lincoln was to be inaugurated. Former president Tyler was elected the presiding officer. All states were invited to send delegates, but by February seven Southern states had already seceded from the Union, and they sent no delegates. As would be expected during that tense period, tempers flared, and delegates had a difficult time even discussing the crisis they faced. They

In 1861, Tyler was elected president of a peace conference in Washington seeking to avoid war between the North and the South. Its recommendations came too late—the Civil War began only weeks after the conference met.

finally drafted a resolution, a sectional compromise remarkably similar to the Missouri Compromise. It was too late, however. As Tyler anticipated, Congress did not approve it.

Tyler returned to Virginia, saddened that the Peace Convention had failed. He now supported secession by Virginia to provide military and economic support for the other states in the new Confederacy. He hoped President Lincoln would pause to think before employing military power against the South. On April 12, 1861, the first shots were fired by South Carolina troops at Fort Sumter, held by Union troops, in the harbor at Charleston. The war had begun.

Tyler and his family became active supporters of the Confederacy. He was elected as a representative in the Confederate Congress. Early in January 1862, he went to Richmond to take his seat in the House. Julia planned to join him one week later. But shortly after he left, she had a dream that he was ill in a bed she didn't recognize. She rushed to the Exchange Hotel in Richmond, where he was staying, and was relieved to find her husband well. Two days later, however, he collapsed in the hotel dining room. Five days after that, on the night of January 17, he began to gasp for air. A doctor was summoned.

When he arrived in the room, Tyler said, "Doctor, I am going."

"I hope not, Sir," his physician replied.

"Perhaps it is best," said Tyler.

Julia gave her husband a sip of brandy. He looked at her, smiled, and died at 12:15 A.M., January 18, 1862. The 71-year-old Tyler died in the bed that Julia swore she had seen in her dream.

Two days later, John Tyler's body was laid in state at the black-draped hall of the Confederate Congress. Thousands of mourners walked by the open casket to pay their respects. The next day a three-mile-long procession of 150 carriages

A photographic portrait of John Tyler in his last years.

followed the hearse to Richmond's Hollywood Cemetery, where Tyler was buried in a grave site next to the grave of former president James Monroe. The cemetery overlooks the James River, the same river that flows past Tyler's beloved Sherwood Forest and his childhood home, Greenway.

In Washington, D.C., during these early days of the Civil War, Tyler was considered a traitor and a Confederate rebel. The Union government refused to take any official notice of his death. Finally, more than fifty years later, in 1915, the U.S. government placed an official monument at Tyler's grave site.

Tyler's Legacy

The last of the Old Virginia aristocracy in the White House, Tyler has long been pictured as one of our weakest presidents. Generally known by Americans only as the "Tyler, too" of the catchy campaign slogan, Tyler's reputation was damaged by the fact that most of the powerful newspapers of the day were operated by pro-Whig factions.

Recently, though, historians have been recognizing Tyler in a more positive light. More than many presidents before or since, Tyler stood for principles he believed in deeply, even when the result was losing the support of his party and of the nation. His belief in a limited federal government represents a strain of thinking that has strong support even today. At the same time, Tyler is remembered for his defense of the presidency. At a time when powerful party and congressional leaders often controlled the president, Tyler insisted that he would exercise the full authority of his office whether or not his party or the Congress agreed. Perhaps his presidency did not succeed because he was too strong, not too weak.

Fast Facts

John Tyler

Birth:	March 29, 1790
Birthplace:	Greenway in Charles City County, Virginia
Parents:	John and Mary Armistead Tyler
Brothers & Sisters:	Older: Anne, Elizabeth, Martha, Maria, Wat Henry
	Younger: William, Cristiana
Education:	College of William and Mary (graduated 1807)
Occupation:	Lawyer
Marriages:	To Letitia Christian (1790–1842), March 29, 1813
	To Julia Gardiner (1820–1889), June 26, 1844
Children:	(see "First Lady Fast Facts" at right)
Political Party:	Democratic-Republican; Whig; Democratic
Public Offices:	1811–1816 Member of Virginia House of Delegates
	1816–1821 Member of U.S. House of Representatives
	1823–1825 Member of Virginia House of Delegates
	1825–1826 Governor of Virginia
	1827–1836 U.S. Senator
	1841 Vice President of the United States
	1841–1845 Tenth President of the United States
	1861–1862 Member of the Confederate Congress
His Vice President:	None
Major Actions as President:	1841 Vetoed two bills to establish a national bank
	1842 Signed the Webster-Ashburton Treaty, fixing the U.S.-Canadian border from Maine to the Rocky Mountains
	1843 Protected the Sandwich Islands (Hawaii) from foreign intervention
	1844 Treaty of Wanghai, opening U.S. trade with China
	1845 Signed the Postal Reform Act
	1845 Signed resolution annexing Texas to the United States
Firsts:	First vice president to succeed to the presidency on death of the president
	First president to have a resolution of impeachment introduced against him
	First president whose wife died while he was in office
	First president to marry while in office
	First (and only) president to be expelled by his own party while in office
Death:	January 18, 1862
Age at Death:	71 years
Burial Place:	Hollywood Cemetery, Richmond, Virginia

Fast Facts
Letitia Christian Tyler

Birth:	November 12, 1790
Birthplace:	New Kent County, Virginia
Parents:	Robert and Mary Brown Christian
Education:	Schooled at home
Marriage:	To John Tyler, March 29, 1813
Children:	Mary (1815–1848) Elizabeth (1823–1850)
	Robert (1816–1877) Anne Contesse (b. 1825, died in infancy)
	John (1819–1896) Alice (1827–1854)
	Letitia (1821–1907) Tazewell (1830–1874)
Firsts:	First president's wife to die during his term of office
Death:	September 10, 1842
Age at Death:	52 years
Burial Place:	Cedar Grove plantation, New Kent County, Virginia

Julia Gardiner Tyler

Birth:	May 4, 1820
Birthplace:	Gardiners Island, New York
Parents:	David and Juliana McLachlan Gardiner
Education:	Tutored privately; attended Madame Chagaray's Institute, New York City
Marriage:	To John Tyler, June 26, 1844
Children:	David Gardiner (1846–1927) Lyon Gardiner (1853–1935)
	John Alexander (1848–1883) Robert Fitzwalter (1856–1927)
	Julia (1849–1871) Pearl (1860–1947)
	Lachlan (1851–1902)
Firsts:	First to marry a president during his term of office
	First to donate a portrait of herself to the White House
	Established practice of playing "Hail to the Chief" when a president appears at state functions
Death:	July 10, 1889
Age at Death:	69 years
Burial Place:	Hollywood Cemetery, Richmond, Virginia

Timeline

1790	1801	1807	1809	1811
Born in Charles City County, Virginia	Thomas Jefferson begins first of two terms as president	Tyler graduates from the College of William and Mary	James Madison takes office as president; Tyler begins practicing law in Charles City County, Virginia	Elected to Virginia House of Delegates; William Henry Harrison defeats Shawnees at Battle of Tippecanoe

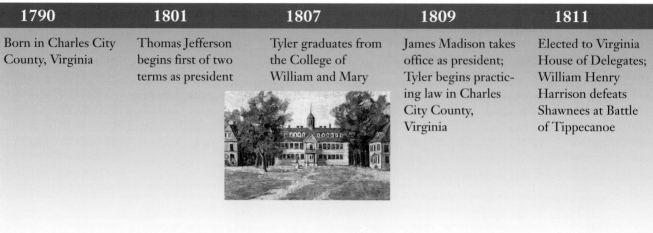

1820	1821	1823	1825	1826
Missouri Compromise passes; Tyler votes against it	Resigns his seat in the House of Representatives	Elected to Virginia House of Delegates	John Quincy Adams elected president, takes office in March; Tyler elected governor of Virginia	Tyler elected to U.S. Senate; delivers eulogy on Thomas Jefferson

1842	1843	1844	1844	1845
Webster-Ashburton Treaty signed, fixing the U.S.-Canada border; Tyler's wife Letitia dies	Warns Britain and France not to intervene in the Sandwich Islands (Hawaii)	Signs Treaty of Wanghai with China, opening trade between the two countries; marries Julia Gardiner; advocates annexation of Texas	Democrat James Polk elected president; Tyler returns to the Democratic party	Signs bill for annexation of Texas, March 1; leaves office March 3 and retires to Sherwood Forest plantation; Texas and Florida admitted to Union as states

1812	1813	1815	1816	1817
War of 1812 begins between U.S. and Great Britain	Marries Letitia Christian at Cedar Grove plantation, Virginia	Andrew Jackson defeats British force at New Orleans; Treaty of Ghent ratified, ending the War of 1812	Elected to the U.S. House of Representatives; takes seat in December	James Monroe takes office as president

1828	1834	1836	1840	1841
Supports Andrew Jackson for president; Jackson elected	Opposes Jackson, joins the Whig Party	Martin Van Buren elected president; Tyler resigns from Senate; Texas declares independence from Mexico	Whigs nominate Harrison for president, Tyler for vice president; Harrison and Tyler win election	March, Harrison inaugurated; April, Harrison dies and Tyler succeeds to presidency; Tyler vetoes two Whig bills to establish Bank of the U.S.; his cabinet resigns

1846	1848	1860	1861	1862
U.S. declares war on Mexico	Mexico surrenders, cedes vast territory to the U.S.	Abraham Lincoln, candidate of the anti-slavery Republican party, is elected president; South Carolina secedes from the Union	Tyler serves as presiding officer of the Peace Convention, February; Civil War begins, April; Tyler elected to the Confederate Congress	Tyler dies January 18 in Richmond, Virginia

Glossary

★ ★ ★ ★ ★

annex: to add a parcel of land to a political unit; the United States annexed Texas in 1845

attorney general: in U.S. government, the official responsible for enforcing federal laws

constituents: the people in a political district whom an elected official represents

nullify: in U.S. history, for a state to declare a federal law unconstitutional and refuse to obey or enforce it

override: in U.S. government, for the Congress to pass a bill into law after the president has vetoed it; the vetoed bill must be passed by a two-thirds majority in both the House and the Senate (*see also* **veto**)

secede: in U.S. history, for a state to withdraw from the United States

tariff: a tax on goods that are imported into a country

veto: in U.S. government, for a president to refuse to sign a bill passed by Congress (*see also* **override**)

Further Reading

American Heritage. *The American Heritage Book of the Presidents and Famous Americans*, Volume 4. New York: Dell Publishing Company, 1967.

Blassingame, Wyatt. *The Look-It-Up Book of Presidents*. Revised edition. New York: Random House, 1996.

Chidsey, Donald Barr. *And Tyler Too*. Nashville: Thomas Nelson, 1978.

DeGregorio, William A. *The Complete Book of U.S. Presidents*. New York: Barricade Books, 1993.

Ferry, Steven. *John Tyler: Our Tenth President*. Chanhassen, MN: The Child's World, 2002.

Kane, Joseph Nathan. *Presidential Fact Book*. New York: Random House, 1998.

Sullivan, George. *Mr. President: A Book of U.S. Presidents*. Revised edition. New York: Scholastic, 1997.

Walker, Jane C. *John Tyler: A President of Many Firsts*. Blacksburg, VA: McDonald & Woodward, 2001.

Welsbacher, Anne. *John Tyler*. Edina, MN: ABDO Publishing Company, 2000.

MORE ADVANCED READING

Chitwood, Oliver Perry. *John Tyler: Champion of the Old South*. Revised edition. Newtown, CT: American Political Biography Press, 2000. (Original edition, 1939.)

Gunderson, Robert Gray. *The Log-Cabin Campaign*. Lexington: University of Kentucky Press, 1957.

Morgan, Robert J. *A Whig Embattled: The Presidency Under John Tyler*. Hamden, CT: Archon Books, 1974.

Peterson, Norma Lois. *The Presidencies of William Henry Harrison and John Tyler*. Lawrence: University Press of Kansas, 1989.

Seager II, Robert. *And Tyler Too: A Biography of John and Julia Gardiner Tyler*. New York: McGraw-Hill Book Company, 1963.

Places to Visit

★ ★ ★ ★ ★

The Capitol Building
Constitution Avenue
Washington, D.C. 20510
(202) 225-3121

Hollywood Cemetery
The burial place of John and Julia Gardiner Tyler, President James Monroe, and other notable people of Virginia.

412 South Cherry Street
Richmond, Virginia 23220
(804) 648-8501

Sherwood Forest Plantation
The home of John and Julia Tyler. The grounds are open to visitors.

14501 John Tyler Highway
Charles City, Virginia 23030
(804) 829-5377
http://www.sherwoodforest.org

Virginia State Capitol
Take a tour of the Capitol, where John Tyler served as governor.

Capitol Square
Richmond, Virginia 23219
(804) 698-1788

White House
Visit the Executive Mansion, where Tyler and his family lived 1841–1845.

1600 Pennsylvania Avenue
Washington, D.C. 20500
Visitors' Office: (202) 456-7041

White House Historical Association
740 Jackson Place NW
Washington, D.C. 20503
(202) 737-8292

Online Sites of Interest

★ **The American President**

http://www.americanpresident.org

Provides valuable information on the life and times of U.S. presidents. Originally prepared from material for a public television series on the president, the site is now managed by the University of Virginia.

★ **The American Presidency**

http://gi.grolier.com/presidents/

This site provides biographical information on the presidents at different reading levels, based on material in Scholastic/Grolier encyclopedias.

★ **Internet Public Library, Presidents of the United States (IPL POTUS)**

http://www.ipl.org/ref/POTUS

Excellent information on presidents and their careers. Especially valuable for its links to other sites with biographies and research resources.

★ **Sherwood Forest Plantation**

http://www.sherwoodforest.org/

The official site about the home of John Tyler. Provides information on the tenth president, his family, and his home. Virtual tour of the plantation and many links to other sites of interest.

★ **The White House**

http://www.whitehouse.gov/history/presidents

The White House site offers brief biographies of each president and first lady. There are also many features on the White House today and the current president.

Table of Presidents

	1. George Washington	2. John Adams	3. Thomas Jefferson	4. James Madison
Took office	Apr 30 1789	Mar 4 1797	Mar 4 1801	Mar 4 1809
Left office	Mar 3 1797	Mar 3 1801	Mar 3 1809	Mar 3 1817
Birthplace	Westmoreland Co, VA	Braintree, MA	Shadwell, VA	Port Conway, VA
Birth date	Feb 22 1732	Oct 20 1735	Apr 13 1743	Mar 16 1751
Death date	Dec 14 1799	July 4 1826	July 4 1826	June 28 1836

	9. William H. Harrison	10. John Tyler	11. James K. Polk	12. Zachary Taylor
Took office	Mar 4 1841	Apr 6 1841	Mar 4 1845	Mar 5 1849
Left office	Apr 4 1841•	Mar 3 1845	Mar 3 1849	July 9 1850•
Birthplace	Berkeley, VA	Greenway, VA	Mecklenburg Co, NC	Barboursville, VA
Birth date	Feb 9 1773	Mar 29 1790	Nov 2 1795	Nov 24 1784
Death date	Apr 4 1841	Jan 18 1862	June 15 1849	July 9 1850

	17. Andrew Johnson	18. Ulysses S. Grant	19. Rutherford B. Hayes	20. James A. Garfield
Took office	Apr 15 1865	Mar 4 1869	Mar 4 1877	Mar 4 1881
Left office	Mar 3 1869	Mar 3 1877	Mar 3 1881	Sept 19 1881•
Birthplace	Raleigh, NC	Point Pleasant, OH	Delaware, OH	Orange, OH
Birth date	Dec 29 1808	Apr 27 1822	Oct 4 1822	Nov 19 1831
Death date	July 31 1875	July 23 1885	Jan 17 1893	Sept 19 1881

5. James Monroe	6. John Quincy Adams	7. Andrew Jackson	8. Martin Van Buren
Mar 4 1817	Mar 4 1825	Mar 4 1829	Mar 4 1837
Mar 3 1825	Mar 3 1829	Mar 3 1837	Mar 3 1841
Westmoreland Co, VA	Braintree, MA	The Waxhaws, SC	Kinderhook, NY
Apr 28 1758	July 11 1767	Mar 15 1767	Dec 5 1782
July 4 1831	Feb 23 1848	June 8 1845	July 24 1862

13. Millard Fillmore	14. Franklin Pierce	15. James Buchanan	16. Abraham Lincoln
July 9 1850	Mar 4 1853	Mar 4 1857	Mar 4 1861
Mar 3 1853	Mar 3 1857	Mar 3 1861	Apr 15 1865•
Locke Township, NY	Hillsborough, NH	Cove Gap, PA	Hardin Co, KY
Jan 7 1800	Nov 23 1804	Apr 23 1791	Feb 12 1809
Mar 8 1874	Oct 8 1869	June 1 1868	Apr 15 1865

21. Chester A. Arthur	22. Grover Cleveland	23. Benjamin Harrison	24. Grover Cleveland
Sept 19 1881	Mar 4 1885	Mar 4 1889	Mar 4 1893
Mar 3 1885	Mar 3 1889	Mar 3 1893	Mar 3 1897
Fairfield, VT	Caldwell, NJ	North Bend, OH	Caldwell, NJ
Oct 5 1830	Mar 18 1837	Aug 20 1833	Mar 18 1837
Nov 18 1886	June 24 1908	Mar 13 1901	June 24 1908

	25. William McKinley	26. Theodore Roosevelt	27. William H. Taft	28. Woodrow Wilson
Took office	Mar 4 1897	Sept 14 1901	Mar 4 1909	Mar 4 1913
Left office	**Sept 14 1901•**	Mar 3 1909	Mar 3 1913	Mar 3 1921
Birthplace	Niles, OH	New York, NY	Cincinnati, OH	Staunton, VA
Birth date	Jan 29 1843	Oct 27 1858	Sept 15 1857	Dec 28 1856
Death date	Sept 14 1901	Jan 6 1919	Mar 8 1930	Feb 3 1924

	33. Harry S. Truman	34. Dwight D. Eisenhower	35. John F. Kennedy	36. Lyndon B. Johnson
Took office	Apr 12 1945	Jan 20 1953	Jan 20 1961	Nov 22 1963
Left office	Jan 20 1953	Jan 20 1961	**Nov 22 1963•**	Jan 20 1969
Birthplace	Lamar, MO	Denison, TX	Brookline, MA	Johnson City, TX
Birth date	May 8 1884	Oct 14 1890	May 29 1917	Aug 27 1908
Death date	Dec 26 1972	Mar 28 1969	Nov 22 1963	Jan 22 1973

	41. George Bush	42. Bill Clinton	43. George W. Bush
Took office	Jan 20 1989	Jan 20 1993	Jan 20 2001
Left office	Jan 20 1993	Jan 20 2001	—
Birthplace	Milton, MA	Hope, AR	New Haven, CT
Birth date	June 12 1924	Aug 19 1946	July 6 1946
Death date	—	—	—

29. Warren G. Harding	30. Calvin Coolidge	31. Herbert Hoover	32. Franklin D. Roosevelt
Mar 4 1921	Aug 2 1923	Mar 4 1929	Mar 4 1933
Aug 2 1923•	Mar 3 1929	Mar 3 1933	**Apr 12 1945•**
Blooming Grove, OH	Plymouth, VT	West Branch, IA	Hyde Park, NY
Nov 21 1865	July 4 1872	Aug 10 1874	Jan 30 1882
Aug 2 1923	Jan 5 1933	Oct 20 1964	Apr 12 1945

37. Richard M. Nixon	38. Gerald R. Ford	39. Jimmy Carter	40. Ronald Reagan
Jan 20 1969	Aug 9 1974	Jan 20 1977	Jan 20 1981
Aug 9 1974★	Jan 20 1977	Jan 20 1981	Jan 20 1989
Yorba Linda, CA	Omaha, NE	Plains, GA	Tampico, IL
Jan 9 1913	July 14 1913	Oct 1 1924	Feb 11 1911
Apr 22 1994	—	—	—

• Indicates the president died while in office.

★ Richard Nixon resigned before his term expired.

Index

About the Author

Betsy Ochester is the author of *Carrie Chapman Catt* (Harcourt/Time for Kids Readers, 2002), *Moving the Lighthouse* (Harcourt/Time for Kids Readers, 2002), *and Great Smoky Mountains National Park* (Harcourt/Time for Kids Readers, 2002). In addition, she has published six titles in the two Highlights for Children's series *Which Way USA?* and *Top Secret Adventures* (1999–2000) as well as dozens of puzzles, stories, and articles for young readers. Ms. Ochester is a graduate of Cornell University. She lives in New York City, only a few blocks from the church where John Tyler and Julia Gardiner were married in 1844.

Acknowledgments

The author would like to extend thanks to Frances Payne Bouknight Tyler, Kay Montgomery Tyler, and Christine Crumlish Joyce, of Sherwood Forest Plantation, for their time, enthusiasm, and answers.